MW00415528

I'M GLAD I DID

I'M GLAD I DID

*Do what it takes not to say
"I should have."*

Sheryl Isenhour

ISBN-13: 978-1546689713

ISBN-10:1 546689710

TABLE OF CONTENTS

1

When They Can No Longer Care for Themselves

> *Love begins by taking care of the closest ones—the ones at home.*
>
> ~ Mother Teresa

"Once a man, twice a child" has been said for many years and will continue to be a valid saying. When a child is born, it is dependent upon someone else for everything that is necessary to sustain life. As they grow and mature, they are then able to care for them-selves and become fully functional adults, but all too often, the adult will revert to their childlike attitudes, actions and inability to function independently of others. This is caused by natural aging, illnesses, and health conditions such as stroke, heart attack, dementia and Alzheimer's disease, just to name a few.

Close relationships with family members are a gift and should not be taken for granted. When parents, relatives or friends reach their elder years, they become even more precious. If time gives you the privilege of seeing your parents and family members reach their elder years, consider yourself one of the lucky ones. Some look at it as a chore rather than a chance to have time with them that many others do not get. They can have illnesses that require you to attend to them on a daily basis or a healthy body with a failing mind. You never know until the time comes what you will face with your loved ones. When we were young, taking care of our parents was not something that we thought about, but now the time is here.

Do you plan to keep them at home? Will you hire someone to take care of them, or will you place them in a facility? I had to make all of these decisions over the years, and I hope I can give you some insights. One thing you never want to say is "I wish I had."

I never knew that I would begin "raising parents" at the age of twelve and that it would last for over fifty years of my life. I took care of my parents, Jerry's parents, stepparents, and his aunt and uncle.

2

The Day that Life Changed

*One of the ways we communicate
That we can be trusted is in the
way we care for other people.*
~ Zig Ziglar

It became a juggling act that I just
accepted. Between full-time careers,
marriage, children, homes, and aging
parents, the balls added up one by
one. I just kept tossing them in the air
as my life filled up, praying they
wouldn't come crashing down on my
head.

Although the days were busy and
the workload always growing, caring

for my father was one of these wonderful experiences that taught me that life doesn't end when a person can no longer relate to what goes on around them. It is never easy to see the person we know slip into a world that only exists behind their eyes. They are breathing, their heart is beating, but in this moment and in our eyes, their mind is not working.

One Sunday morning my life took a drastic turn. Seconds would begin turning into minutes, minutes into hours, hours into days, days turned into weeks and weeks into months. This is how it went for me at the age of thirty-five.

I had just finished breakfast with my children when I got a call from my mother wanting me to come talk to my father. Now I don't know about you, but when I was young, this was never a good sign. This time was to be worse than anything I could have ever imagined.

I put the kids in the car and headed to their house. When I walked into the den, Dad was extremely pale and had cupped his face with his hands. I got down on my knees in front of him and pulled his fingers back. He was disoriented and didn't seem to realize I was even there. Finally, after calling out to him several times and asking what was wrong, he told me that his head hurt badly. Dad was never one to complain so I knew it was more than just a headache.

This was totally not like him. He was extremely intelligent and had a clarity about him that to me was almost superhuman. He never kept notes, but he never forgot anything, unlike most of us. He could do math faster in his head than I could do on a calculator. Actually, I never saw him use one. He would do quotes on house constructions in his head as I would add them on my calculator, and then he would wait for me to catch up with him before he would give me the total. I had often told him that I wished I had his mind. Now I look back and see how fast what you have can be taken away.

After realizing it was not within my powers to help Dad, I knew it was time to contact a doctor. Since it was Sunday I wasn't sure what to do. Did I call the doctor or take him to the hospital? Being from a small town and being friends with our family doctor, I had his personal number and decided to call him for assistance. I called and was relieved when I got an answer. He suggested that Dad and I meet him at the office. I immediately put my father into the car and made him as comfortable as possible. My mom did not think that there was a lot to worry about, and she chose to keep the kids with her at home, letting me take Dad alone.

We reached the office in about fifteen minutes, and by this time, Dad was bent double in the car, grasping his head with all his strength. It was hard for him to focus. His vision was blurry, and he was getting anxious. Alan helped me get him on the table at the office, and after only a few minutes, he explained that we needed to get to the hospital in Concord to run a test that he was not able to do at the office. We put Dad back into the car, and Alan followed us to the hospital. He had already informed them we were on the way, and they were waiting on us. We were taken directly in and immediately sent for a CT scan.

Shortly after the scan, Dad and I

Were put into an ambulance headed to Presbyterian Hospital in Charlotte. The only explanation was that they found some areas in the scan that they did not like. I called my mom and told her she should meet us there as soon as she could find someone to watch the kids.

Time stood still in the ambulance. As I looked toward the back of the ambulance, they were putting IVs into Dad and doing what they could to calm him. They looked at me, and I knew they wanted me to say some - thing to him. They cut the siren off just long enough for me to speak loudly so that Dad could hear me, and I assured him that he was in good hands and I was there. I was near tears, wanting to get back there to him but because of regulations, I had to stay strapped in. I felt so helpless.

Upon getting to the hospital, I was face with people more worried about insurance than about the man lying on the stretcher. I know hospitals have rules, but where was the compassion? While I was frantically telling them that I had not had any time to get the paperwork, they were denying treatment to my father. Dr. Brawley, who was soon to be Dad's chief neurosurgeon, came in. He told everyone except me and his nurse to get out and leave us alone, and that he would take full responsibility for getting it worked out.

He talked with Dad for a few minutes, asked me a lot of questions, and told the nurses to get us upstairs for more scans and then to ICU. Again, we were bombarded with staff wanting to see insurance cards. Again in a much angrier tone they were told to do what he said and to leave us alone. This is when time sped up. Time was not our friend. I was informed that surgery was set for 6 AM the next morning. Mom got to the hospital about this time, and after bringing her up to speed, I went back to trying to comfort my father.

Visiting hours were over in ICU, and Mom said we ought to go home. This was not going to happen. I called my children, explaining to them how much I loved them but that I needed to stay with their grandfather. I asked Mom to have someone bring me some clean clothes in the morning and to make sure the children were taken care of. Mom left and there was a sense of being totally alone as I curled up on a chair in the waiting room.

I could only spend so much time in the ICU with Dad, and the rest of the time I sat in the waiting room and prayed. I made several calls to the kids before bedtime to make sure they were okay and that they understood why I was not home. It never ceases to amaze me how children can understand when it's necessary. I didn't know how much they would have to take me at my word for the next several months.

3

When Time Stands Still

Pieces of our past slowly slip away, but it's the things that make time stand still that make us sane.

~ Unknown

Morning slowly came, and Dad's nurses and doctors began arriving. I was surprised and relieved that Dad was to have a full team of surgeons in the operating room with him. One doctor took his time to explain things a little more clearly to me while the others prepped for the surgery. They had located two aneurysms, one

On either side of the brain, and since they were not able to cut the skull on both sides, they would have to open up where one was located and work their way around and through his brain to get to the other. Both were at the point of rupturing, and so there was no time to waste. Suddenly I was alone again, but I knew in my heart that Dad was in the best of hands.

They had taken Dad back early before anyone else had time to get there. My mother, brother, and grandmother got there shortly after they wheeled him into the operating room. Everyone began to pace the waiting room, but I just found a quiet corner and sat there. I needed to work out my emotions. I soon realized that someone was going to have to assume the strong position, and it did not take much time to realize it was going to have to be me.

Hours passed. Nurses would come out and assure us that the doctors were doing all they could do. Finally, Dr. Brawley slipped out for a minute only to tell us that they were nowhere near knowing the outcome of the surgery. He explained that he would not be back until it was over. He wanted to be there for my dad and me. That was all that mattered.

For some unknown reason I was still calm. *Did I know it was not his time to go?* After what seemed like an eternity, Dr. Brawley and several doctors came out. Dad, as they said, skirted death three different times during the surgery, and the next several hours would be critical.

Again, time stood still. Hours later, they moved him back to the ICU unit that would be his home for the next fifteen weeks. Night drew near, and again, I was going to have to make the choice of staying at the hospital or returning to my children. Over the next weeks, my kids and I would not have a lot of time together, so there had to be quality time. I made the decision not to bring them to the hospital for several weeks due to the bandages, Dad's lack of responsive - ness, and the fact they were too young to go into ICU and could only see him through the window.

After continually staying at the hospital, except for the times I went home for a shower and a few minutes with the kids, they started letting me stay with Dad. I did not have to leave at the end of visiting hours as others did.

4

The Mind, Totally Unpredictable

Expect the best. Prepare for the worst. Capitalize on what comes.

~ Zig Ziglar

Several days passed before they let Dad wake up. Once awake it was apparent that he did not know me as his daughter. He didn't remember anything that had happened. He knew none of the family. We were told that this should return in time, but there was no time line to follow.

As he began to stay awake longer,

23

He knew my name but not the person he associated with his daughter. But I would take whatever I was given. We became good "friends." I was the girl who helped him with what he needed.

I began taking care of many of my father's needs—bathing and feeding him—so the nurses could tend to the medical needs of other patients. Even though he did not know me as a daughter, we were getting closer, and he would talk to me and no one else. I became the communicator between him and the staff.

Finally, he improved enough to get moved out of ICU, which posed a whole new series of problems. He was no longer sedated as much, and with his mental status where it was, he did not understand instructions. He still had a feeding tube, and there was no way that he was going to leave it alone. After pulling it out several times, they made the decision to restrain him. You have no idea how hard it is to watch a man be tied down. It is torture. Sometimes, I could talk him out of pulling it out during the day, but the night was not so easy.

After he pulled it out several times and they had to replace it, his throat was getting raw. I decided the best thing was to sit beside his bed, tie his hands to mine, and sleep there. When he moved, I was able to wake up and take care of his needs, that is, if I went to sleep at all.

He grew more coherent now that he was not sedated, and we began having some long conversations about the time he thought he was living in. The past was clear. The present was only the moment we were in at any second. We spent a lot of time back in World War II, discussing what was going on there.

At times, I was a nurse, and at other times, I was one of the people in his platoon. I was whatever he needed me to be at that moment. At other times, we were building houses. Dad had built houses from the time he left the army until the day we ended up at the hospital.

One day, Dr. Brawley walked in when I was standing across Dad in the center of the bed, swinging my arms upward. I was asked what, if I didn't mind him asking, I was doing. Dad quickly said, "She is hanging sheetrock, and if you will shut up, she can finish." Dr. Brawley chuckled and shook his head. He said it amazed him that I would do whatever it took to keep Dad calm. But what else did I have to do?

Many days when I needed a break or wanted a few minutes to read the

Medical books the nurses had
brought on how the brain works, I
would pretend to knock over the nail
bucket, and he was content as
long as I sat on the floor to pick them
up. Another day, the doctor walked
into the room with Dad getting ready
to strike a lighter, not a problem
except for the oxygen he was on.

After Dr. Brawley nearly had a
heart attack, I told him not to worry.
It wouldn't light, didn't even have a
striker. You see, my dad had smoked
all his life, and now he had been
operated on, tied up, lost his dignity
and more, I had decided that he
should be able to think he could
smoke. I had stopped at the store that
morning after going home for clean
clothes and picked up a lighter, a
carton of cigarettes, straws exactly
the size of cigarettes, some glue,
scissors and a razor blade. I cut the

bottom of the box open, then the bottom of the cigarette packs and then removed the cigarettes. I replaced them with straws cut to the exact length of his cigarettes and stuffed them with cotton so they would not bend. I glued the packs shut and then the box. I placed the carton back into the bag from the store, along with the lighter with no fluid or striker, and gave them to him.

The excitement I saw in his face made me keep this up for the remainder of his stay. I left the hospital with two Ziploc bags full of "cigarettes" when his stay was over. I would not dare reuse the straws since the box and packs would not look perfect. But what else did I have to do?

Once they removed the feeding tube and he could eat real food, we spent many meals and many hours with "a bite for you, a bite for me." By this time, the nurses were bringing me food from the cafeteria so I could work with Dad to get him to eat. I was doing most of the daily care other than changing IVs and giving meds.

Dad was having alternating good and bad days, but at least he was alive and we could work with that. We had been in ICU for fifteen weeks, and now we were headed toward our tenth week in a regular room.

They had taken him off IVs and put him on oral meds. The powers that be were at the point of kicking him out of the hospital. Not sure what it would be like with him at home, Mom began preparing the house for his release from the hospital. He still did not know Mom, my brother, or me. Over the past weeks, he had been telling them he did not know who they were, and he wanted them to leave. Needless to say, I was not one of their favorite people since he was telling them I was the only one he wanted there. Such is life.

5

Time to Go Home

*If light is in your heart, you will
Find your way home.*
                              ~ Rumi

The day before they were to
release him, Dad had this strange
look on his face. He looked at me in a
way I had not seen over the last
twenty-five weeks. He called me by
name and asked how Lori and David,
rather Cute and Hardrock, his
grandchildren, were doing. Tears
began to flow, and even though Dad
did not know why, he cried with me.
The time came to leave. We packed

Up our things, and Dad, Mom and I
headed down the road toward home.

Dad still did not recognize my
mother, which made the ride rather
long. She did not understand why he
didn't know her. As we pulled out of
the parking lot onto the road, my dad
began screaming to pull over. I
steered to the side of the road to see
what was happening, and he was
shaking. I asked him what was wrong,
and he just kept saying we were
going to hit something.

I assured him we were not, and we
pulled back onto the road again, for
him just to resume the screaming.
Mom was in the back screaming at
him because he was screaming. So
we stopped once again. Not sure of
what was going on, I convinced
Dad to put his hands over his eyes
and lay his head back. Several times
on the way home, he would remove

his hands, and we would go through it again. I was never so happy to see their driveway.

I was sure life was headed back to normal now, but it wasn't to be so. We pulled up in front of the house, and Dad turned to me and asked, "Who lives here?" Unable to convince him that he was home, I told them to stay in the car and I would be right back. I opened the door to the house and went in. Upon my return a minute later, I told him that the owners of the house had suggested that we stay there for a few days until he was stronger. It was hard to convince Mom to play the game, but finally, she had no choice and went along with it.

After getting Dad settled and fixing them some lunch, I proceeded to finish making the house ready for Dad to move around. The evening went on, and I noticed that when Dad had to go to the bathroom, he headed in the wrong direction. Then when he went to the bedroom to lie down, he did the same. This concerned me, but I had an idea I wanted to explore.

After he had had a good nap, I sat down beside him and asked him if he could draw the floor plan to his house. In the years prior to his surgery, we had spent many hours drawing floor plans that he would use to build spec houses. I gave him a piece of paper, and he drew the house totally inverted from the one we were sitting in. It was then that I realized what was right for most of us was left to him, thus his fear of cars being on the wrong side of the road on the way home.

Dad had been home for several days when one morning he woke up and headed in the right direction. The mind had put right and left back into their place. The next day he remembered my mother and several days after that, my brother.

We were on our way to a semi-normal life again. Dad never got all his short-term memory back, and he never regained any memories from that Sunday morning when it all started until after he was home for over a week. This remained a total void in his memory. But I did have memories, wonderful but hard memories.

Another thing that I had now was a time in his life that he and I could talk about—the army. We had things to talk about that he had never told anyone else. This had been a time in his life that he refused to talk about with my mother or anyone else.

I think I was given this time to get to know the man I admired more than anyone else in the world. These are the times you treasure.

After making it through all this, Dad was not to live but a more years. He was diagnosed with Stage IV cancer and passed away in six short weeks after diagnosis, but that is another story.

6

Why This Direction in Life

In life you can say, I should have or I'm glad I did.
~ Self

It's because of times like these that I coach people to know that the bad times can be their best times. Life has its way of turning disaster into something marvelous. Do not feel sorry for me, but rejoice that I was given the time to get to know my father and say the things that I needed to say that would one day be forever lost to death.

I became a coach, a trainer and a

public speaker to let people know that they do not have to go through these times alone. If I had had someone to talk to during this time, and others that followed, it would have helped me to understand that what I was going through was not just my journey but one that others had taken, also. Therefore, one of the avenues I have chosen is to coach and train in the field of taking care of aging parents. You see, this was just the beginning of my raising parents.

After marrying Jerry and acquiring his parents, stepparents, aunt, and uncle, I had many more experiences. Before becoming an empty nester at sixty-two, I had experienced the single parenting of my two children, aneurysms, cancer, heart attacks, diabetes, dementia, Alzheimer's, alcoholism and just plain old age. I had full-time businesses while doing this, and with it all going on, my immediate family turned out great.

The juggling act became a normal part of life, and I do not regret any ball that I juggled. Life makes many turns, but how you deal with them is what makes it special. The realization is that you do not have to do it alone. You want to be able to say, "I'm glad I did" instead of "I wish I had."

* * *

Thank you for taking your time to read one of my stories. As you make your journey, I wish each of you will realize you are not alone. Remember the past, enjoy the present, and look to the future with hope.

ABOUT THE AUTHOR

Sheryl Isenhour has been known as the problem solver and go-to person her whole life. She has been a single mother of two children She has nursed and cared for elderly parents, both her own and her in-laws, until they passed. She developed her drive and inner strength doing everything from becoming the caretaker of her mother and their home at the age of twelve to surviving personal and business trials. She tested the male-dominated fields, from driving semis and limos to building a wallcovering business in times when women were supposed to stay at home. She has been an active participant and keeper of the books in multiple successful family businesses. Sheryl built two successful businesses prior to becoming CEO of a successful outdoor living manufacturer, IBD Outdoor Rooms. In that role, she has proven herself to be an accomplished designer and a recognized expert in the field of outdoor furniture and living areas. Through her talks, inspiration and assistance, she has coached others to find success in their own life goals and pursuits, and she might just be the resource you need when your dreams seem out of reach!

Tom Ziglar, head of Ziglar Coaching and one of Sheryl's coaches, says, "Sheryl Isenhour is proving to be one of our most valued Ziglar Legacy Certified trainers and coaches. She showed intense interest in adopting the training associated with her certification as both trainer and one

On one success coach, growing our confidence in her commitment. We realize the Ziglar standard for legacy trainers and coaches is unique to the industry, and it's rewarding and encouraging to have Sheryl represent the Ziglar brand. She offers her own professional style of integrating the Ziglar philosophy with her delightful personality and ability to identify with others. Our confidence in Sheryl Isenhour is surpassed only by her heartfelt desire to contribute to the lives of those she touches with the timeless message." Life has a way of presenting each of us with failures. You know, those roadblocks that block our travels to our dreams when life so often throws a curve ball.

Sheryl lives by the John Maxwell creed of always falling forward, turning failures into successes, time after time in her own life, and she helps others when they face these challenges. As Vince Lombardi shared, "The winner is the person who gets up when they are knocked down." She is a winner who has been known all her life as the one to help others get back up after they have been knocked down! That true grit comes from the person who inspired her in life ... her father!

In this lifelong process, Sheryl has learned the delicate art of balancing one's professional life with the duties and responsibilities of one's family life. She did it, when at an all too young age, she faced her father's declining health. She overcame her own business and personal obstacles and turned them into success stories. Some may say she is a survivor, but in reality, she is a creative problem solver who works tirelessly and persistently to make things happen and remove roadblocks to success. In other words, she has already done what many spend their lives hoping to accomplish. Remarkably, she keeps giving to others without expectations of rewards!

Sheryl has a true gift in her ability to assist people with their challenges, that sacred duty of taking care of family members as they age. She has dealt personally with the issues of dementia, Alzheimer's disease, alcoholism, heart issues, aneurysms and cancer, along with the emotional issues that are associated with the problems of aging loved ones. She understands this journey is easier if you have someone there to help guide you through some of these problems and will be there for you. Unless this person has faced these issues personally, it is hard for them to really provide that help so often needed—you see she understands what you are feeling!

Sheryl also understands the challenges that working with your family in business present to your personal life. She has walked the walk, so she can talk the talk. Having worked with husbands, children and other family members, she understands the difficulty so many face in making the required decisions in business that must be made while not disrupting the family unit. A tall order, but one she has experienced and one she continues to build her skills to coach on.

You know the feeling, we all get it at times. The wall is up, it blocks your path. The challenges of life and the stress that is carried from your business life hover over you like a storm that will not blow away. It blocks your happiness at home with your loved ones and the ability to take care of your responsibilities. Sheryl understands, but more than that Sheryl can share with you the processes to get past the obstacles that block your path and hinder you from reaching your dreams. Today her passion and motivation is to bring her attitude, experience, and deep knowledge of business and life to the service of others. It is her joy to help others be successful in every phase of their lives. This ability has been enhanced along the way in such high-powered training courses as the Zig Ziglar Legacy Certification and Ziglar Coaching Certification. Traing under Larry Winget and Suzanne Evans has given Sheryl the ability to share her story with others from the stage. But, as Sheryl will tell you, her greatest teacher has been life, and the business of life itself.

For more information on Sheryl Isenhour's coaching, speaking and seminars, visit sherylisenhour.com or call 704-425-0211.

■■■■■■■■■■■■■■■■■■■■■■■■■■■■■■■

Feel free to contact her via email at sheryl@sherylisenhour.com. She can answer any additional questions and determine if she is the right person for you or your company.

Made in the USA
Columbia, SC
26 February 2018